AF615916

The Wheel

Also by Jordan Jones

Poetry

Sand & Coal: Poems
Futharc Press / 1993

Selections from The Wheel
Obscure Publications / 2004

Translations

The Anti-Heaven, Part 1, by René Daumal
Obscure Publications / 2003

The Anti-Heaven, Parts 2 & 3, by René Daumal
Obscure Publications / 2004

Mugle by René Daumal
Leaping Dog Press / forthcoming / 2005

The Wheel

Poems

Jordan Jones

Front cover photograph, "Cogs" by Don Carstens, © 2005 Brand X Pictures. Used by permission. Book design and title page photo editing by Jordan Jones. Cover design by Linda Zupcic. Author photograph by John Hagman.

The author wishes to thank the following for their comments on these poems while in manuscript: Ellery Akers, Francisco X. Alarcón, Greg Boyd, Kirpal Gordon, Sandra McPherson, and Robert Peters. Additionally, the author thanks his fellow founding editors at The 365 Project: Greg Boyd, A.D. Liano, and Richard Martin. Paul Rosheim of Obscure Publications graciously supported this work by publishing a chapbook of selections.

Special thanks are due to Eric Paul Shaffer, without whose friendship and support this book would never have been completed.

Some of these poems appeared previously in the following publications:

Tamafyhr Mountain Poetry	"Porn Bomb"
The 365 Project	"Cool to be Stupid" "Ball-and-Chain Affair" "Naked in Babylon" "Lima Beans" "Birds of Iraq" "Temporary Empire"
The Nambuli Papers	"Manifesto"
What Book!?	"Zen Baker"

ISBN 1-58775-020-1
Library of Congress Control Number: 2005901963

Printed on acid-free paper by McNaughton & Gunn
in the United States of America.

FIRST EDITION

Leaping Dog Press
PO Box 3316
San José, CA 95156-3316
www.leapingdogpress.com

"Publishers of contemporary literature with bark and bite,
as ecstatic as the leaping dog."

Contents

iii ::: Full

iv :::: Waning

The Wheel

for those who care
& those who need them to

for the shamans who
return us to a place of origins

Manifesto

Thales, the pre-Socratic philosopher, said that "Everything is water," or he may have said, "Everything comes from water," "Water delivers all births," or "Water is the center of all things." Actually, it's unclear exactly what he said, as we only have Aristotle's summary, but it's critical to understand that the planet is tidal and watery by nature.

Water flows into, over, through, up, down, around, and within the tallest and the smallest trees of the forest. Even mammals live by the tide of blood; the body is a watershed.

Write in nature, and nature will erase any attempt at personal immortality. Whether you write in the sand of an estuary and allow your work to perish completely submerged, or you search out the mountain forests to do your writing in the wild, words are liquid we pour onto the earth.

A day will come when those who walk upright will attempt symbol languages, creating messages from sticks, rocks, leaves, feathers, scat, rubbish, and carcasses. These artworks will decay, blow away, be scavenged by raccoons, grasshoppers, wolves, and vultures, and otherwise return to the natural state of the world, that is to say, the cycle of revolution, contagion, degradation.

i : New

Cycle

The sun eats the flesh of the moon.
The moon makes a dress of the stars.

On earth, we have nothing more
to take care of than ever —

Just each other —
that is enough.

Stonehenge

Circle around circle around horseshoe
        — the star enters the horseshoe's open mouth,
a gate into the smiling world, a vulva,
        slick with morning dew.

To map the sky
        through all its turning cycles,
        the arborists carved massive
columns from stone,

& rolled the liths
        over the loamy earth
        mile by mile
on hewn trunks of alders.

        The columns aligned
the stars & sun & moon
        in all precision.

The Druids learned the great circle
    of weather & seasons
opens & closes
    like the bells of four o'clocks,
without inventing paper & ink,
    mathematics & physics.

No less wise, no less foolish
    than the other inventions,
stands the solid circle
    amid heather & bracken.

Fingerprints

The whirl of years in wood,
the whorls on the tips
of our fingers,
are relief maps to where we've been /
where we're going.

Circles bisect circles at the sawmill.
The state collects our finger whorls
in a dactyloscopy of electrons
circling like carrion birds,

The state & the sawmill only seem
to stop our history in its tracks /
because the tracks remain —

The state & the sawmill
will one day be fossils of little interest,
all straight lines & human planning,
not a biological circle
to be found.

Turkey Day

I saw Iron Eyes Cody
stuffing a turkey
into a jug marked XXX,

to return to a time
before Columbus
separated the Arawok
from their hands,

before the Pilgrim promise
to "make this continent
a marsh of blood,"

before despair summoned
the Ghost Dance,
a diminishing ring of steps
to make the White Men
disappear.

Holy Disc of Quetzalcoatl

Among the Aztecs, the wheel & axle
were sacred objects —
the calendar, the earth's spin
made visible.

Only toy leopards,
sleek with playfulness,
rolled the holy disc of Quetzalcoatl —

*   *   *   *

In the absence of oxen, horses, camels,
the disk blazed golden, holy,
while laden porters
bore unwheeled carts from sea
to palace.

For every openness to the sacred,
every obeisance to the sun,
moon, and the lathe-turned sky,

comes a balancing brutality,
blindness, & butchery.

Children, bored, dragging their rolling toys
behind on string,
abandon the play of the sun & heavens,
impatient to learn the earthly play
of men who people graves.

Orpheus in the Underworld

When Orpheus in the Underworld struck his lyre
& sang Euridice back to life,

he bore music into a place that before
had only known silence & sounds of anguish.

Cerberus relaxed his watch & cocked
three heads at three angles to listen.

Sisyphus rolled his stone to a rest
& leaned on it to listen.

Even the spinning of Ixion stalled,
& transfixed by more than the wheel,

head down, he gazed
into dimness to listen.

Prometheus raised his head to listen.
The vulture at his liver leapt
into the air to perch atop a crag.

Even the Furies halted their sisterly
destruction & wept.

Orpheus sang his wife to life,
but Hades knew this singer would look back —

if only to be certain —
& lose it all.

Four-Faced Messengers of God

"The appearance of the wheels and their work was like unto
the colour of a beryl; and they four had one likeness:
and their appearance and their work
was as it were a wheel in the middle of a wheel."
— Ezekiel, 1:16

Wheels of flame
with four four-faced messengers,
ox, man, lion, & eagle,
on four wings each,
flew from amber north,
hooved, and the color of brass,
spoke the *Book of Revelation*
in cacophonous animal symphony.

Each wheel within a wheel
turned, both aflame,
carrying the chariot of omniscience.
The four-headed beasts were covered with eyes.

This is how we learn what to hear:

> Satan's menagerie has no demons as fantastic as God's.
> The devil's illusions are that your day job matters,
> that it's important to yell at your girlfriend, that she needs
> to walk away hurt. The demon sticks to mundane illusions
> so close to the skin that you wouldn't know the difference.

The deity wants to shake you from these delusions and say:

> "What goes on is constantly wheeling into flame.
> Pay attention to each moment.
> Trust your blood.
> Get all this down.
> I am at the right hand
>   & the left.
>
> "You have seen Brahma,
> You have seen Shiva,
> You have seen Vishnu,
> I am no different, the alpha & omega.
> Pay attention, pay attention,
>   don't turn away."

No Moon

I saw the eclipse of no moon —

with clouds between me
& the moon as it came into shadow,
the sky was uniformly dim;

the partial glow of streetlights
ignited the dull haloes
of a dozen paltry moons.

*   *   *

Behind the clouds, & seen all over the clear globe
in these latitudes & nighttime hours,
the moon put on the pj's of our planetary shadow,
hoping to get some rest from always turning
the same side toward the gazing earth.

The respite was brief,
but no doubt sweet.

ii :: Waxing

Sanborn Park

Pale green leaves underfoot,
maroon of madrone,
ochre of tanoak on the trail —

hundreds of small, slippery poems
the trees address
to the leisure
of summer soil.

Decaying leaves nourish wildness
in the terrain Coyote inhabits, just outside
the circular edge of the urban.

Open Fields

Simi Valley, 1975–1985

At twelve, my friends & I ran
north of town
into fields of grass —
paper crinkling in the summer heat,
past where Dominic, the Basque shepherd, drove his flock.

The Frog Pond —
sheen of oil, repository for the Chrysler
junk heaps of suburbia —
where we gathered flint & tried
to chip arrowheads
with blunt force, aching
for the natural life —
away from apron strings
& TVs, asphalt & classrooms.

We dreamt of curling up at night
in a fire-cored shell of eucalyptus.

Dominic led his sheep
    north from Madera Road to Pyramid Hill
& back,

since then, his route has been blocked by body shops,
    by the KardKey plant,
        & the rushing stream of California 118.

We measure our loss
    by remembering
        a child's larger, wheeling world.

Backyards

i.

where we stoke the barbecues,
where the last owl falls dead
                    from its perch in the palm,
sudden, stiff, splayed onto the patio.

From any yard you can see
the new furniture factory, smell
          "the smell of money"
finishing the air,
          the final turned leg of a table —
Early American.

ii.

In the sudden porch light,
            a possum tries to stare me to death.

Tomorrow, holed up in the Walkers' garage,
            baring her teeth,
                        she'll be shot for rabid
by the SPCA.

                        Dead, she and her pocket children
will turn out to have been clean.

Armed to the teeth,
                        we have nothing
            to fear.

Matthew

What he searches for is as fixed as he is,
        & fades as he arrives.

Thousand Oaks to Pine Barrens, Boulder
        to Katmandu
                via Tokyo, Hong Kong, Bangkok . . .

In Oregon now to buy land,
        root himself,
                        learn to farm
without a plow,
        he tosses clay-
                        covered seed into clover:
               tends, irrigates, harvests.

As the taproot pushes deeper, wandering
        leaches out of him.

He trades the wild rootlessness
he can no longer use
for a rooted wildness —

water, nourishment, a sense of place —

that tangles the soil with roots
& slows *his* erosion.

The corn seed he scatters in a field of rye
takes hold of his earth
& gives it a future,

which,
being a body,
he could never offer.

Zen Baker

He who bakes bread
shall know grain by touch
& blood of fiber

shall expand his heart
as he leans to knead.
Dough, secret & liquid,

shall rise toward the hot stoves
of his hands, teaching him
to breathe, to press & pull a loaf

into shape from within
as he dances without.
He shall hide behind his apron

a belly of knowledge,
rounded alike by deep brown
successes & burnt failures.

The Color of Fireflies

Ellanore C. Lawrence Park

In the Disney version
of the South,
fireflies are white

tiny bulbs strung through the trees
in the eternal Christmas
of a southern summer evening.

Today, I saw the real color
of fireflies toward twilight:
whitish green, nearly transparent,

like the green flash I saw
on 'shrooms in
Eureka.

The color of fireflies
resists all attempts to recall it
& refuses to remain.

Night Grapefruit

The possum, seeking the night
grapefruit, runs along the brick wall
then drops into the yard
near the tree
of sour meat.

He sucks his fill
of pink & pulp.

The motion detector light
freezes him
in sight of my cat, Natasha.

Each of them,
wild & tame
— in its own manner —
stares into the eyes of the other.
They do not move.

Under dim stars &
brilliant porch light,
under the balcony of wood,

they sniff & back away,
return to animal caution —

No human yard
contains them;
no human wall
keeps them out.

Chimney Tree

Big Basin Redwoods State Park
8 August 2004

The hollowed-out trunk
of the chimney tree
shows the path —

standing inside the base,
I saw sky
through & beyond
the center of the tree —

let the heartwood burn,
straight through the tree's top,
so long as xylem
& phloem still conduct,

so long as
the remaining trunk
holds:

Here's where death does not consume,
& life differs little from death.

A practice of dying makes a living
wise, long, & sweet.

Valley Oak

We may never know where
the whirpool of the tree —
which started with a jay hiding an acorn
& forgetting where —
ends, & the circle
of earth, water, & sky begins.

The Body is a Watershed

I am only a temporary geology of bones
water sands to fluid curves,
speeding its return to itself
& the expanding acres of krill.

Water moves through me & falls away —
as charged with minerals as I am,
as salty, as polar.

Oxygen carves rivulets through my flesh
& feeds the soil of each drinking cell.

Water wheels back into the air
from whoever I am
to fish, fowl, protozoan, person.

How joyous to be a mortal house
of rushing water! —
to be at the center, all my life,
of the give & take of water & clay.

iii ::: Full

Bird Flu

The birds of Asia are sick
                              & dying.

Earth spins not toward progress
          but toward pandemic

The Bengal tigers in Sriracha Tiger Park
          have been shot by their keepers.

Blue pheasants & black swans,
          clouded leopards & white tigers;
the net is cast wide & wider,

wide enough, we fear, to catch us all.

Cool To Be Stupid

You gotta lean into cool,
                    it ain't gonna lean
into you.
              You gotta mean what you
                    mean
while you can.

                    Slice across the grain
of any snow day. The ages of your life,
like rings in a tree,
                    forget nothing:

days spent sick, watching 30-year-old
              re-runs on TV Land,
flying down the hill on a toboggan
              on a weekday ....

What the tree rings show is how aware
              the tree needed to be.

Sometimes, it's the quick who are dead.

Dr. Platt's Homeric Essay Assignment

"I will be in my office at 4 a.m.
    The door will be locked.

"Slide your papers
        under the door
just as 'the child of morning,
            rosy-fingered Dawn,'
gleams through my office window.

"Your essays must be 1,250 words long.
        Not 1,251, not 1,249.

"Oh, and make one sentence perfect:
    beautiful, crystalline, pure.

"Don't tell me which one it is."

Rinse Cycle

I watch Audrey Hepburn
                        burn for William Holden
            in *Sabrina,*
as the dishes
            rinse in the background.

One of them is naïve,
            one worldly. Neither knows
which is which.

By the end of the movie,
            they've traded
neuroses.

            She's learned
how to make a soufflé.
            He's nearly gotten fired
from the family business.

And she's dumped him
          just as he gets
interested,
          in order to date his older,
wiser, more sensible brother,
Humphrey Bogart.

          I told you it was a movie.
The dishes are dry.

21 October 2002

Ball-and-Chain Affair

When she saw what I was packing
how could she refuse?

We were bugs in lust,
humping like we had just two weeks to live:

a fortnight of bliss,
with a ball-and-chain in my pocket

to make it work. But somehow, someone says
I'm filthy. Somehow, I need the censor

to black me out, to hide what
makes my brief span so sweet.

And now, they want to build a mall
in the last field any of us know,

They scoff, "Endangered species!
with a schlong like that

how could they be endangered?"
Up go the bug zappers,

& there goes the neighborhood.
It's punishment

enough to provoke
a plague.

This ain't the last
you've seen of *my* ball-and-chain!

Naked in Babylon

"Imagine Mr. Bush, nude, addressing, addressing the State of the Union.
Oh, and imagine also Saddam Hussein, nude, addressing his people.
Now what? You know."
— Nadine Gary, Raelian Protester

Naked in peace and war.

Naked at night
& in the day.

Naked on the battlefield:
shorn of gas masks
& shoulder-launched ordnance;
naked of boots & packs.
Lost in the desert naked.

Naked in the dust storms
of Babylon.

We enter and leave this world
naked. Naked at first;
naked at last!

* * *

Protestants, Jews & Muslims,
ashamed of being naked,
cover up their bodies
like the bodies of the dead —
first in palls,
& last under naked earth.

The living gather final
handfuls of the remaining earth
first to hurl at one another,

& later use to mourn
& take leave of their own.

Language for the Body

I shuffled 7 years in shoes of forgetfulness,
only to awake as from a coma, needing rehab
& counseling.
                    The other sleepwalkers,
in various stages of drowse & dream,
stubbed their toes, rubbed their eyes.
                              Some of them grinned at me.

          I doubted the shapes
of the shadows on the wall, disbelieved the money
could do this, unbelieved the fear of no money
could do this.

                    I no longer possessed
                              a language for the body,
or a body, just an alimentary canal, feeding
& eliminating as required by the economy.
                              I was blind, deaf
          & in all ways sliced from the art
                                        of the daily:

I don't know who I was
          impersonating, except
to say, "Myself."

And so
I began
to be.

19 & 20 October 2002 / 1 December 2002

What Goes Around ...

i. Flora Belle Sees Thelma Wearing Lipstick for the First Time

"Thelma, your mouth
looks like a hen's ass
in chokeberry season."

ii. Different

My grandfather Lawrence,
    jitterbugged to his knees at last,
    asked for Thelma's hand.

Her mother Faye said: "I think 16
is a little young to get married,
    don't you?"

Lawrence said to Thelma:
"Sixteen? You told me you were *eighteen."*

& Thelma said to her mother:
"You were sixteen
when *you* got married."

"Well, things were different
back then —"

iii. Beer Run

At 10, my father spent the summer
in Huntington with his grandmother Faye
& her mother Flora Belle.

Flora Belle drank
on the sly,
& knew her daughter
disapproved —

Faye — thin as an altar rail —
was advised by her doctor:
"I know you're against drinking,
but to put on some weight,
drink a beer every day."

So that day, Faye called my father inside.
"Carl, go down the corner store,
& get me a bottle of beer,
& *don't* tell your grandmother."

& Flora Belle pulled my father aside.
"Carl, now I want you to do me a favor,
but you *can't* tell your grandmother —"

Carl took the nickels he saved
& bought two beers of his own.

He didn't tell either grandmother.

4–10 January 2004

iv :::: Waning

Porn Bomb

for Al Franken
who reported the paranoid fear of porn bombs
in the arriving George W. Bush administration

arms akimbo, naked
in feigned delight,
severed from moaning
pouts, in a cloud of
diesel smoke & concrete
dust, on top of crushed
Republicans in business
suits of Italian manufacture,
taken unawares by terrorism of the porn
variety, unleashed by the Al Qaeda
of Clintonian degradation, with statues of justice
blind & naked for centuries —

it's as if those Democrats have no shame
of the body at all

El Toro

for A. G.

"The 47th annual El Toro Air Show ended with record-setting crowds of more than 2 million over the weekend who made a final salute to an Orange County tradition that has thrilled spectators over nearly five decades."
— Los Angeles Times

Stars rip
clouds from the sky
tonight, —

Allen joins Jack
& Neal
in eternity.

Stealth
bombers & Blue Angels no longer
scorch the dusty circus
air of El Toro —

the great angry bard flies
to join his Buddha-
body.

Fujimori says we've reached
the end of history.
El Toro Air Base goes under padlock.

Allen
on the far shore, watches Charon pole his skiff
back across the black waters.

Paper soldiers in secret rooms
map out the next
terrible war.

27 & 29 April 1997

Lima Beans

"If some would like to turn this into class warfare, I, that's not how I think: I think about the overall economy."
— President George W. Bush

The lines for free food in Lima,
Ohio, stretch half way
                    around the block.

Just after Christmas, your unemployment
insurance dried out
like the tree you couldn't afford
                    but bought anyway.

          Standing in line, you imagine
Ken Lay's mansion.
                    The greed pyramid
& millions of simple
                    retirements, like yours,
collapsed and burnt in Manhattan.

When you return home, your TV
shows flashy graphics of “Crisis
                    in the Gulf,” the sequel,
but there’s no class
                    warfare in the mind
                    of the President.
Aren’t you glad?

Birds of Iraq

"In the name of peace, if he does not disarm,
I will lead a coalition of the willing
to disarm Saddam Hussein.
— President George W. Bush

The President is afraid
that the oil of Saddam
might go up in plumes
& what that will mean for the economy
of the Iraq to come —

So add to the human loss,
the smoke of the oil of wealth
smudging the air of birds.

Who thinks of the sooty falcon,
the rustic bunting, the common babbler,
the ring ouzel, & red-breasted merganser,
& all the other birds of Iraq?

Who thinks of the people of Iraq?
War after war after war ....

Iran, Iran, Iran,
US, US, US,
Saddam, Saddam, Saddam:
who thinks of the people of Iraq?

Dead Sea sparrow & dusky thrush,
Black-throated accentor & black francolin,
Brahminy mynah, black stork,
& grey-crowned crane. Pygmy cormorant
meet Levantine sparrowhawk —

> all of you will burn in fires
> programmed in Kansas,
> or, in flight above the burnt earth
> of retreat, choke on the sooty remains
> of your ancestors from the cretaceous:

misery spreads from person to person,
then takes to the air,
like a virus in reverse.

Temporary Empire

"92 million Americans will keep, this year,
an average of almost $1,100 more of their own money."
— President George W. Bush

The calculus of tax and spend
        is not so much math as spin.

Who's going to keep my $30,000 in debt?
        The government keeps it for you, don't fret.
And who's going to pay for replanting the forests?
        Let the shade of concrete buildings refresh you.
$200 billion for a pre-emptive war?
        Don't worry! The final accounting will appear
on your toe tag.

When will the bacchanal collapse in sparks & shattering glass?
When will the Huns ride in
        to gather our waste for food,
        to survive on what we 'doze into holes in the land?

One day, doubtless before geological time
gets to it, the Statue of Liberty will hold her lamp
    slightly above the rising waters;

all the bills will be overdue, all the good faith & credit
    of the United States will be on the sunken side
of the flood, & the spin will be seen
    at last
for what it has been:

lies that fueled the engine of power,
    the temporary Empire.

While it lasted, it was the greatest
    party on Earth.

Leaping Dog Press, *featuring* Asylum Arts Press

Applebaum, Samuel. ***Chtcheglov: Poems.*** Asylum Arts.
Applebaum, Samuel. ***Judea Capta: A Long Poem.*** Asylum Arts.
Aufderheide, Charles. ***Garden of Games: The Collected Poems of Charles E. Aufderheide.*** Asylum Arts.
Basso, Eric. ***Accidental Monsters: Poems & Texts, 1976.*** Asylum Arts.
Basso, Eric. ***Bartholomew Fair: Fiction.*** Asylum Arts.
Basso, Eric. ***The Beak Doctor: Short Fiction, 1972–1976.*** Asylum Arts.
Basso, Eric. ***Catafalques: Poems, 1987–1989.*** Asylum Arts.
Basso, Eric. ***The Catwalk Watch: Poems, 1977–1979.*** Asylum Arts.
Basso, Eric. ***Enigmas: Short Plays, 1979–1982.*** Asylum Arts.
Basso, Eric. ***Ghost Light: Poems, 1990–1994.*** Asylum Arts.
Basso, Eric. ***The Golem Triptych: A Dramatic Trilogy.*** Asylum Arts.
Basso, Eric. ***The Sabattier Effect: with incidental music composed & arranged by the author.*** Asylum Arts.
Basso, Eric. ***The Smoking Mirror: Poems, 1980–1986.*** Asylum Arts.
Baudelaire, Charles. (Kendall Lappin, translator) ***Echoes of Baudelaire: Selected Poems.*** Asylum Arts.
Bernard, Kenneth. ***The Baboon in the Nightclub: A Poem.*** Asylum Arts.
Bernard, Kenneth. ***How We Danced While We Burned, followed by La Justice, or The Cock That Crew: Two Plays.*** Asylum Arts.
Bernard, Kenneth. ***The Qui Parle Play & Poems.*** Asylum Arts.
Boyd, Greg. ***Carnival Aptitude: Being an Exuberance in Short Prose and Photomontage.*** Asylum Arts.
Boyd, Greg. ***The Double: Doppelangelgänger: An Annotated Novel.*** LDP Book #4.
Boyd, Greg. ***The Nambuli Papers: A Multimedia Novel.*** LDP Book #6.
Boyd, Greg. ***Water & Power: Stories.*** Asylum Arts.
Cull, Mark E. ***One Way Donkey Ride: Short Fiction.*** Asylum Arts.
Daumal, René. (Jordan Jones, translator) ***Mugle: A Novella.*** LDP Book #8. Forthcoming in 2005.
Dixon, Stephen. ***Friends: More Will and Magna Stories.*** Asylum Arts.
Fondation, Larry. ***Common Criminals: L.A. Crime Stories.*** Asylum Arts.
Hendershot, Cynthia. ***City of Mazes and Other Tales of Obsession.*** Asylum Arts.
Hood, Charles. ***The Xopilote Cantos.*** Asylum Arts.
Jones, Jordan. ***The Wheel: Poems.*** LDP Book #11.
Kostelanetz, Richard. ***Minimal Fictions.*** Asylum Arts.
Lappin, Kendall (translator) ***Dead French Poets Speak Plain English: An Anthology of Poetry.*** Asylum Arts.
Lappin, Kendall. ***Memoirs of a Translator of Poetry.*** Asylum Arts.
Lappin, Kendall (translator). ***The Muse Spoke French: An Anthology of Poetry.*** Asylum Arts.
Martin, Joe. ***Parabola: Shorter Fictions.*** Asylum Arts.
Martin, Richard. ***Marks: Poems.*** Asylum Arts.
Martin, Richard. ***Modulations: Poems.*** Asylum Arts.
Martin, Stephen-Paul. ***The Gothic Twilight: Short Fiction.*** Asylum Arts.

Martin, Stephen-Paul. ***Instead of Confusion: Fiction.*** Asylum Arts.

Nerval, Gérard de. (Kendall Lappin, translator) ***Aurélia followed by Sylvie: Fiction.*** Asylum Arts.

Papadimitrakopoulos, Elias. ***Toothpaste with Chlorophyll & Maritime Hot Baths: Stories.*** Asylum Arts.

Peters, Robert. ***Mad Ludwig of Bavaria & Other Short Plays: Drama.*** Asylum Arts.

Peters, Robert. ***Poems: Selected & New 1967–1991.*** Asylum Arts.

Peters, Robert. ***Where the Bee Sucks: Workers, Drones and Queens of Contemporary American Poetry.*** Asylum Arts.

Redonnet, Marie. (Gilbert Alter-Gilbert, translator) ***Dead Man & Company: Poems.*** LDP Book #7.

Redonnet, Marie. (Jordan Stump, translator) ***Understudies: Stories.*** LDP Book #9.

Richman, Elliot. ***Franz Kafka's Daughter Meets the Evil Nazi Empire!!!: The Heroism of Roaches: Holocaust-tainted Poems.*** Asylum Arts.

Richman, Elliot. ***Honorable Manhood: Poems of Eros & Dust.*** Asylum Arts.

Richman, Elliot. ***The World Dancer: Poems.*** Asylum Arts.

Roditi, Edouard. ***Choose Your Own World.*** Asylum Arts.

Romero, Norberto Luis. (H. E. Francis, translator) ***Last Night of Carnival & Other Stories.*** LDP Book #5.

Shaffer, Eric Paul. ***Lāhaina Noon: Nā Mele O Maui: Poems.*** LDP Book #10.

Shaffer, Eric Paul. ***Living at the Monastery, Working in the Kitchen: Poems.*** LDP Book #3.

Shaffer, Eric Paul. ***Portable Planet: Poems.*** LDP Book #1.

Stoloff, Carolyn. ***You Came to Meet Someone Else: Poems.*** Asylum Arts.

Mark Wisniewski. ***All Weekend with the Lights On: Stories.*** LDP Book #2.

Leaping Dog Press books are available in fine bookstores everywhere, on the Internet at leapingdogpress.com, Amazon.com, BN.com, and Borders.com, or by contacting:

Leaping Dog Press
PO Box 3316
San José, CA 95156-3316

When ordering direct, include $3 for the first book, and $1.50 for each additional book for shipping. California residents should add 8.25% sales tax.

Leaping Dog Press books are distributed to the trade through:

Biblio Distribution, Inc., an NBN Sister Company
4501 Forbes Blvd., Suite 200
Lanham, MD 20706

Web:	bibliodistribution.com	E-mail:	custserv@nbnbooks.com
Phone:	(800) 462-6420	Fax:	(800) 338-4550

Photograph by John Hagman

About the Author

Jordan Jones is the author of *Sand & Coal,* published by Futharc Press in 1993. His poetry, fiction, non-fiction, and translations have appeared in *The American Book Review, Asylum, The Boston Book Review, Fiction International, Heaven Bone, The LA Reader, The Review of Contemporary Fiction,* and *Small Press,* as well as in the anthologies *Anyone Is Possible: New American Short Fiction* (Red Hen Press, 1998) and *What Book!?: Buddha Poems from Beat to Hip Hop* (Parallax Press, 1998). In 2004, Obscure Publications published *Selections from The Wheel.*

His translations of René Daumal's poetry collection *Le Contre-Ciel* appeared in two volumes from Obscure Publications in 2003 and 2004. His translation of René Daumal's novella *Mugle* is forthcoming in 2005.

He was co-editor of *The Northridge Review* and poetry editor of *California Quarterly,* and founded *Bakunin* (1990–1997), a literary magazine "for the dead Russian anarchist in all of us." In 2003, he co-founded and co-edited the online multimedia collaborative art exhibit, The 365 Project, (the365project.org). He is currently the editor and publisher of Leaping Dog Press and Asylum Arts Press.

He lives in the Coyote Creek Watershed of Santa Clara County, California.